Cross Stitch

Samplers

2

8

From traditional to modern, you'll find the perfect sampler for your home.

12

15

20

LEISURE ARTS, INC. • Maumelle, Arkansas

The Pedigree of Honey

A sweet yet eloquent poem by Emily Dickinson takes center stage in this gorgeous old-fashioned sampler. Worked in rich, warm tones with a touch of soft pink and purple, it features a host of handsome bumblebees surrounded by a traditional floral vine border.

Designed by Sharon S. Pope

Note: Please read all instructions on page 24 before beginning.

Stitch Count = 142w × 142h

FABRIC

- One 18" × 18" (45.7cm × 45.7cm) piece of 28-ct. Tea-Dyed Linen by Charles Craft (stitched over two threads)

DESIGN SIZE

- 25-ct. = 11 3/8" × 11 3/8" (28.9cm × 28.9cm)
- 28-ct. = 10 1/8" × 10 1/8" (25.7cm × 25.7cm)
- 32-ct. = 8 7/8" × 8 7/8" (22.5cm × 22.5cm)

INSTRUCTIONS

Center the design and begin stitching over two fabric threads. Work cross stitches, half stitches, and quarter stitches with two strands of cotton embroidery floss. Work backstitches with one strand of cotton embroidery floss. Use a pressing cloth to carefully iron the needlework from the back before framing as desired.

THE PEDIGREE OF HONEY
CHART DIAGRAM

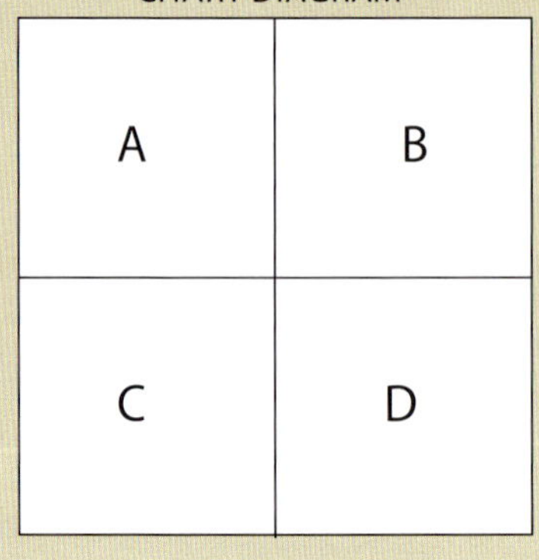

Project Tip

Working with Several Floss Colors

When working with frequent color changes, use several needles to avoid rethreading the same needle over and over. Work a few stitches in one color, bring the needle to the front of the fabric and put it aside. Introduce the next floss color and needle and continue.

AaBbCcDdEeFfGgHhIiJj
The pedigree of honey
Does not concern
the bee;
A clover, any time, to him
Is aristocracy.
EMILY DICKINSON
KkLlMmNnOoPpQqRrSsTt
UuVvWwXxYyZz0123456789

The Pedigree of Honey A

CROSS STITCH

ANCHOR		DMC	COLOR
273	H	535	Very Light Ash Gray
898	M	611	Drab Brown
8581	L	646	Dark Beaver Gray
900	T	648	Light Beaver Gray
891	B	676	Light Old Gold
890	E	729	Medium Old Gold

CROSS STITCH

ANCHOR		DMC	COLOR
275	F	746	Off White
1003	J	921	Copper
1001	K	976	Medium Golden Brown
842	P	3013	Light Khaki Green
871	Q	3041	Medium Antique Violet
870	Z	3042	Light Antique Violet

The Pedigree of Honey B

CROSS STITCH

ANCHOR		DMC	COLOR
888	U	3045	Dark Yellow Beige
262	R	3052	Medium Green Gray
1024	G	3328	Dark Salmon
1013	D	3778	Light Terra Cotta
868	N	3779	Ultra Very Light Terra Cotta

BACKSTITCH

ANCHOR		DMC	COLOR
273	(black line)	535	Very Light Ash Gray
898	(brown line)	611	Drab Brown

Gray area indicates last row of previous section of design.

The Pedigree of Honey C

CROSS STITCH

ANCHOR		DMC	COLOR
273	H	535	Very Light Ash Gray
898	M	611	Drab Brown
8581	L	646	Dark Beaver Gray
900	T	648	Light Beaver Gray
891	B	676	Light Old Gold
890	E	729	Medium Old Gold

CROSS STITCH

ANCHOR		DMC	COLOR
275	F	746	Off White
1003	J	921	Copper
1001	K	976	Medium Golden Brown
842	P	3013	Light Khaki Green
871	Q	3041	Medium Antique Violet
870	Z	3042	Light Antique Violet

The Pedigree of Honey D

CROSS STITCH

ANCHOR		DMC	COLOR
888	U	3045	Dark Yellow Beige
262	R	3052	Medium Green Gray
1024	G	3328	Dark Salmon
1013	D	3778	Light Terra Cotta
868	N	3779	Ultra Very Light Terra Cotta

BACKSTITCH

ANCHOR	DMC	COLOR
273	535	Very Light Ash Gray
898	611	Drab Brown

Gray area indicates last row of previous section of design.

The Joy of Stitching

Designed by Gail Bussi

Most stitchers can remember exactly who it was that first taught them to put needle to fabric. Whether it was a grandma, a mother, or a friend, they all felt the joy of passing along their knowledge for others to treasure. Celebrate that joy with this diminutive sampler.

Note: Please read all instructions on page 24 before beginning.

Stitch Count = 61w × 93h

FABRIC

- One 12" × 14" (30.5cm × 35.6cm) piece of 32-ct. Antique White Belfast® Linen by Zweigart® (stitched over two threads)

DESIGN SIZE

- 32-ct. = 3⅞" × 5⅞" (9.8cm × 14.9cm)

FINISHING MATERIALS

- One 6" × 10" piece of coordinating fabric for backing
- 3 small tassels
- 5" bellpull hanger

GENERAL INSTRUCTIONS

Each band of the sampler is labeled with a number on the chart. Start at the top of the fabric and chart and begin stitching, working down the rows in order. Work all stitches using one strand of Silk Mori thread or DMC® cotton embroidery floss. For rows 2, 3, 11, 14, and 15, refer to the stitch diagrams for detailed instructions on forming these specialty stitches.

FINISHING INSTRUCTIONS

Trim the needlework to 4¾" × 7½", leaving 1½" of fabric above the stitching at the top. Sandwich the needlework and backing fabric with right sides together. Using a sewing machine set to 12 stitches to the inch, sew around the perimeter of the stitching with a ¼" allowance, following the three points at the bottom of the needlework design. Leave the top of the piece open for turning. Trim the corners (being careful to not get too close to the stitching), turn the piece right side out, and press. Zigzag the top opening closed. Turn over the top edge ¼" above the stitching and tack down by hand to create a casing for the hanger. Attach the tassels to the bottom three points.

SHARING THE JOY OF STITCHING
BRINGS OUR HEARTS TOGETHER

CROSS STITCH

DMC		KREINIK SILK MORI	COLOR
3727	A	1092	Lightest Wood Violet
745	Y	2013	Light Gold
819	T	3042	Lightest Dresden Rose
963	H	3044	Medium Dresden Rose
962	V	3045	Medium Dark Dresden Rose
3052	L	4076	Dark Dusty Green
524	I	4203	Light Sage
522	Z	4204	Medium Sage
3743	K	6123	Light Dusty Lavender
3042	O	6124	Medium Dusty Lavender
712	D	7124	Cream

FRENCH KNOT

DMC		KREINIK SILK MORI	COLOR
962	•	3045	Medium Dark Dresden Rose

BACKSTITCHES

DMC		KREINIK SILK MORI	COLOR
962	—	3045	Medium Dark Dresden Rose
3052	—	4076	Dark Dusty Green
3042	—	6124	Medium Dusty Lavender

ALGERIAN EYELET

DMC		KREINIK SILK MORI	COLOR
712	✳	7124	Cream

FOUR-SIDED STITCH

DMC		KREINIK SILK MORI	COLOR
Ecru	□	7126	Ecru

OPEN HERRINGBONE

DMC		KREINIK SILK MORI	COLOR
Ecru	X	7126	Ecru

SATIN STITCH

DMC		KREINIK SILK MORI	COLOR
3727	||||	1092	Lightest Wood Violet
963	||||	3044	Medium Dresden Rose

Stitches You'll Use

(2) Algerian Eyelet

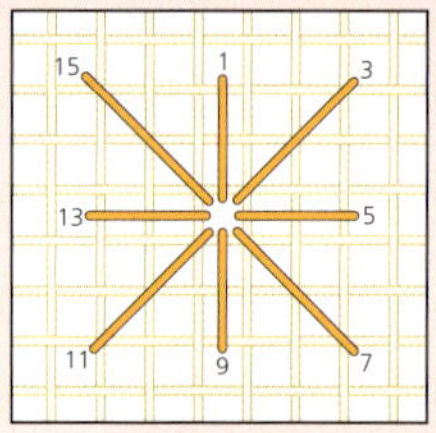

(11) Four-Sided Stitch

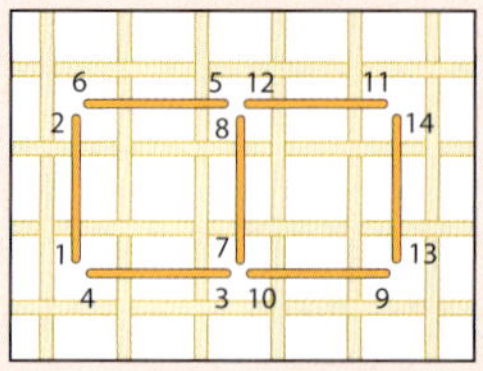

(14) Open Herringbone

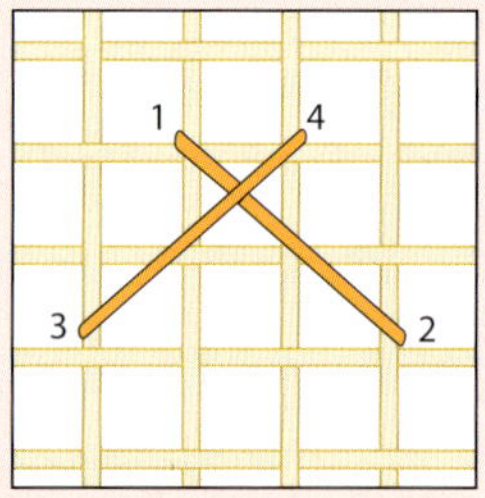

(3) (15) Satin Stitch

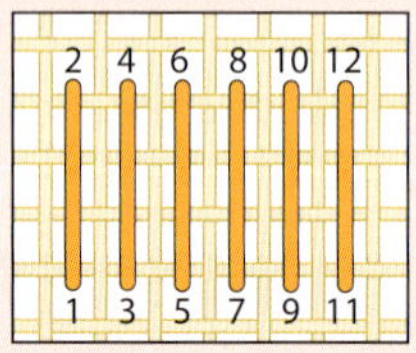

Project Tip

Changing Design Size

Most cross stitch designs can be adapted to different sizes just by changing the thread count of the fabric. To determine the final design size when stitched on a different count of fabric, just divide the stitch count by the thread count. A design that is 100 stitches high will work out be 10" high when stitched on 10-ct. fabric, or approximately 5½" high when stitched on 18-ct. fabric (100 ÷ 18 = 5½"). Remember to use half of the thread count when stitching over two threads on linen or evenweave.

SHARING THE JOY OF STITCHING
BRINGS OUR HEARTS TOGETHER

A Giving Heart

Designed by Alma Lynne Hayden

Show your adoration for your sweetheart with this endearing sampler stitched in sweet pinks and greens.

Note: Please read all instructions on page 24 before beginning.

Stitch Count = 99w × 88h

FABRIC

• One 15" × 15" (38.1cm × 38.1cm) piece of 14-ct. white aida

DESIGN SIZE

• 11-ct. = 9" × 8" (22.9cm × 20.3cm)
• 14-ct. = 7" × 6¼" (17.8cm × 15.9cm)
• 16-ct. = 6⅛" × 5½" (15.6cm × 14.0cm)

INSTRUCTIONS

Center the design and begin stitching. Work cross stitches with two strands of cotton embroidery floss. Use one strand of cotton embroidery floss to work backstitches. Use a pressing cloth to carefully iron the needlework from the back before framing as desired.

CROSS STITCH

ANCHOR		DMC	COLOR
9046	A	321	Christmas Red
266	S	470	Light Avocado Green
265	T	471	Very Light Avocado Green
253	B	472	Ultra Light Avocado Green
302	Y	743	Medium Yellow
1022	P	760	Salmon
1021	L	761	Light Salmon
382	C	3371	Black Brown
035	V	3705	Dark Melon

BACKSTITCH

ANCHOR		DMC	COLOR
267	———	470	Light Avocado Green

Gray area indicates last row of previous section of design.

A GIVING HEART CHART DIAGRAM

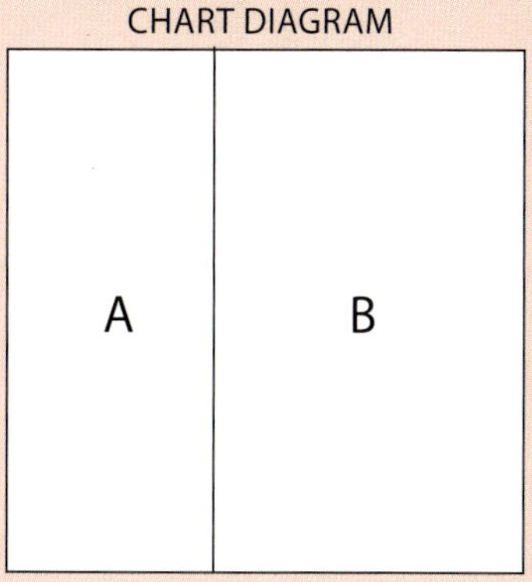

A Giving Heart A

A Mother is Love

Designed by
Ursula Michael

While one day in

May is devoted to showing mothers how much they are appreciated, it is a sentiment that should be shared all year-round. This sampler is the perfect way to show how much you value that special mother in your life.

Note: Please read all instructions on page 24 before beginning.

Stitch Count = 66w × 191h

FABRIC
- One 14" × 18" (35.6cm × 45.7cm) piece of 28-ct. Ecru Linen by DMC®

DESIGN SIZE—SAMPLER
- 25-ct. = 5¼" × 15¼" (13.3cm × 38.7cm)
- 28-ct. = 4¾" × 13⅝" (12.1cm × 34.6cm)
- 32-ct. = 4⅛" × 12" (10.5cm × 30.5cm)

INSTRUCTIONS—SAMPLER
Center the design and begin stitching over two fabric threads. Work cross stitches and quarter cross stitches with two strands of DMC linen or cotton embroidery floss. Use one strand of DMC floss to work backstitches. Use a pressing cloth to carefully iron the needlework from the back before framing as desired.

Instructions for the Bee Ceramic Bowl and Butterfly Handbag Mirror on page 19.

A Mother is Love A

A Mother is Love B

CROSS-STITCH

DMC COTTON FLOSS		DMC LINEN FLOSS	COLOR
162	V	L162	Light Blue
223	Z	L223	Light Dusty Pink
225	N	L225	Pale Shell Pink
415	X	L415	Chrome Grey
435	J	L435	Golden Brown
452	3	L452	Shell Grey
760	T	L760	Salmon
833	O	L833	Golden Olive
902	E	L902	Dark Garnet
967	A	L967	Pale Apricot
3012	2	L3012	Khaki Green
3861	7	L3861	Light Taupe

BACKSTITCHES

DMC COTTON FLOSS	DMC LINEN FLOSS	COLOR
902	L902	Dark Garnet
3012	L3012	Khaki Green

Gray area indicates last row of previous section of design.

A MOTHER IS LOVE CHART DIAGRAM

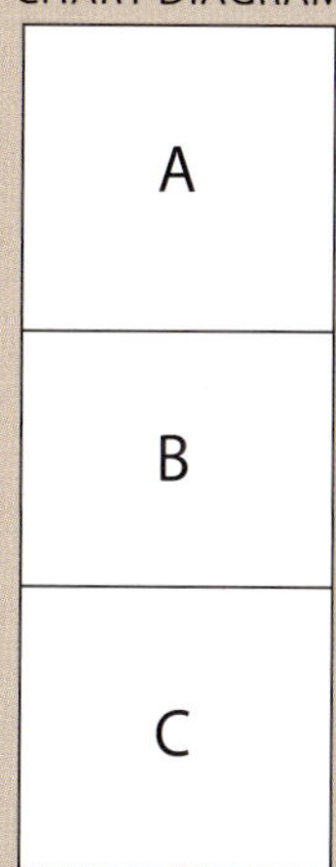

A Mother is Love C

CROSS-STITCH

DMC COTTON FLOSS		DMC LINEN FLOSS	COLOR
162	V	L162	Light Blue
223	Z	L223	Light Dusty Pink
225	N	L225	Pale Shell Pink
415	X	L415	Chrome Grey
435	J	L435	Golden Brown
452	3	L452	Shell Grey
760	T	L760	Salmon
833	O	L833	Golden Olive
902	E	L902	Dark Garnet
967	A	L967	Pale Apricot
3012	2	L3012	Khaki Green
3861	7	L3861	Light Taupe

BACKSTITCHES

DMC COTTON FLOSS		DMC LINEN FLOSS	COLOR
902	—	L902	Dark Garnet
3012	—	L3012	Khaki Green

Gray area indicates last row of previous section of design.

Bonus Projects

FABRIC

• Two 6" × 6" (15.2cm × 15.2cm) pieces of 28-ct. Ecru Linen by DMC®

DESIGN SIZE—BEE CERAMIC BOWL

• 28-ct. = 2" × 1" (5.1cm × 2.5cm)

DESIGN SIZE—BUTTERFLY HANDBAG MIRROR

• 28-ct. = 1³/₈" × 1³/₈" (3.5cm × 3.5cm)

FINISHING MATERIALS—ACCESSORIES

• 3" × 2" pink lidded oval ceramic bowl
• Round handbag mirror with a 2¾" design area

INSTRUCTIONS—ACCESSORIES

Stitch the motifs shown in the sampler, using the same fabric and strands of floss as indicated on page 15. For the lidded bowl, stitch the bee motif from the lower portion of the sampler. For the mirror, stitch any of the three butterfly motifs (the sample shown uses the third butterfly). Use a pressing cloth to carefully iron the needlework from the back before inserting into the accessories according to the manufacturer's instructions.

Stitches of Love

Designed by Gail Bussi

Put a little piece of your heart into every stitch on this darling banner. The touching words remind us of handmade needlework's true magic.

Note: Please read all instructions on page 24 before beginning.

Stitch Count = 60w × 93h

FABRIC

- One 10" × 12" (25.4cm × 30.5cm) piece of 32-ct. Ivory Jobelan® by Wichelt Imports (stitched over two threads)

DESIGN SIZE

- 32-ct. = 3¾" × 5¾" (9.5cm × 14.6cm)

EMBELLISHMENTS

- 1 package of Cream #40123 petite glass seed beads by Mill Hill®

FINISHING MATERIALS

- Fusible web
- 3" × 4¼" piece of ecru wool felt
- 4" bellpull hanging rod and finials
- Cording for hanger
- Matching sewing thread
- Fray Check™ (optional)

GENERAL INSTRUCTIONS

Center the design and begin stitching over two fabric threads. Use one strand of Kreinik Silk Mori, Kreinik Silk Mori Milkpaint, or DMC® cotton embroidery floss to work all stitches. Attach beads with one strand of coordinating thread. Lay the needlework facedown on a terry cloth towel (to protect the beads) and use a pressing cloth to carefully iron the needlework from the back before finishing.

FINISHING INSTRUCTIONS

Trim the needlework to 1" from the edge of the stitching along the bottom and side edges, and 2" from the top edge. (If desired, serge or sew a zigzag stitch on top and side edges to prevent fraying.) Fold back the sides of the needlework fabric at the edge of the stitching and press. Use fusible web to fuse the flaps to the back of the needlework.

To create the points at the bottom of the piece, trim the fabric to ½" from the bottom edge of the stitching. Carefully clip the fabric between the stitched points and fold the excess fabric to the back. Hand-sew the flaps in place, making sure the points are even. You may wish to use a drop of Fray Check™ at the inside corners of the points to prevent the fabric from fraying.

Fold the fabric at the top of the needlework piece to the back twice at the top edge of stitching to form a pocket for the hanging rod. Whipstitch in place with matching thread. Use fusible web to affix wool felt to the back of the piece. Insert the hanging rod into the top pocket and tie cording to form a hanger.

MAY THE LOVE IN OUR HEARTS
BE REFLECTED IN EACH STITCH

CROSS STITCH

DMC		KREINIK SILK MORI MILKPAINT	COLOR
813	U	0553	Medium Colonial Blue

DMC		KREINIK SILK MORI	COLOR
3727	T	1092	Lightest Wood Violet
316	S	1094	Medium Wood Violet
745	A	2013	Light Gold
819	Y	3042	Lightest Dresden Rose
963	R	3044	Medium Dresden Rose
962	K	3045	Medium Dark Dresden Rose
3052	B	4076	Dark Dusty Green
3817	C	4163	Light Victorian Green
3816	D	4164	Medium Victorian Green
524	H	4203	Light Sage
522	E	4204	Medium Sage
3752	N	5053	Light Slate Blue
3743	Q	6123	Light Dusty Lavender
3042	Z	6124	Medium Dusty Lavender

BACKSTITCH

DMC	KREINIK SILK MORI MILKPAINT	COLOR
813	0553	Medium Colonial Blue

DMC	KREINIK SILK MORI	COLOR
3052	4076	Dark Dusty Green
3816	4164	Medium Victorian Green
3041	6126	Dark Dusty Lavender

STRAIGHT STITCH

DMC	KREINIK SILK MORI	COLOR
716	7124	Cream

ALGERIAN EYELET

DMC	KREINIK SILK MORI	COLOR
Ecru	7126	Ecru

CLOSED CHEVRON STITCH

DMC	KREINIK SILK MORI	COLOR
316	1094	Medium Wood Violet

SATIN STITCH

DMC	KREINIK SILK MORI	COLOR
524	4203	Light Sage

BARRIER STITCH

DMC	KREINIK SILK MORI	COLOR
Ecru	7126	Ecru

FOUR-SIDED STITCH

DMC	KREINIK SILK MORI	COLOR
3727	1092	Lightest Wood Violet

BEAD

MILL HILL PETITE GLASS SEED	COLOR
40123	Cream

Stitches You'll Use

Algerian Eyelet

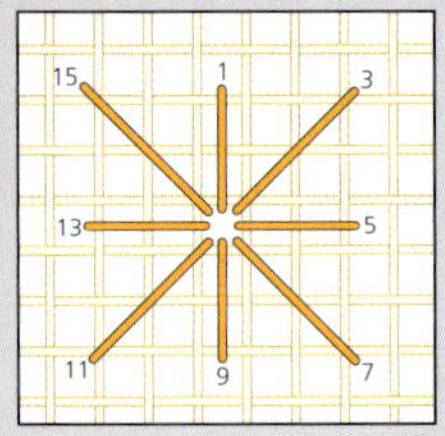

Closed Chevron

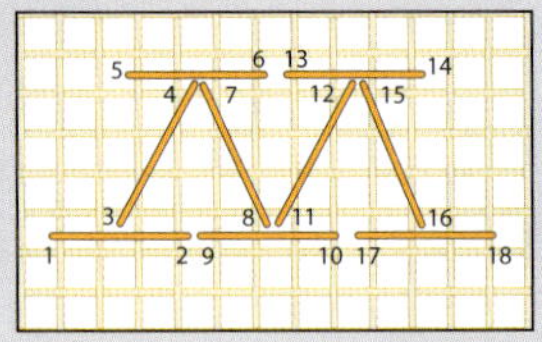

Satin Stitch

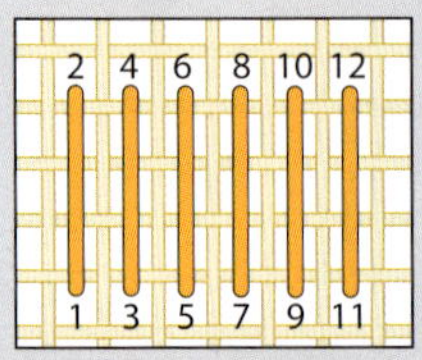

Barrier Stitch

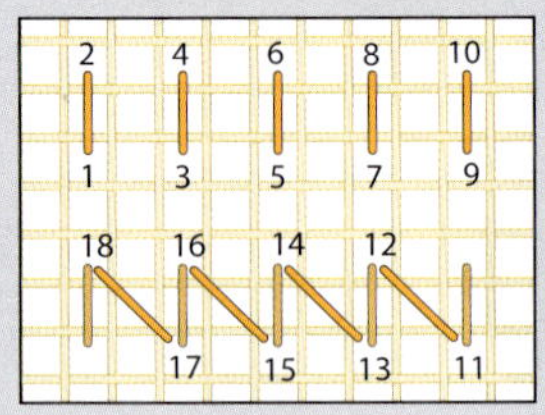

Four-Sided Stitch

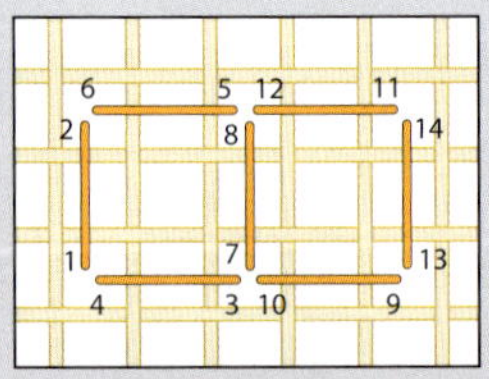

Project Tip

Go With the Grain

By following the grain of embroidery floss, you lessen the wear and tear on your thread as you draw it through the fabric. To find the grain direction, cut a length of floss. Loop the thread over so both the cut ends lie next to each other. Do not allow the two ends to bundle together, as you must be able to differentiate between them. Holding the cut lengths close together, about ½" from the tips, use one finger of your free hand to gently tap the cut ends. Watch carefully—the end that balloons most is the end that should be threaded through your needle (and is the shorter tail).

MAY THE LOVE IN OUR HEARTS
BE REFLECTED IN EACH STITCH

General Instructions

Getting Started

For most projects, the starting point is at the center. Every chart has arrows that indicate the horizontal and vertical centers. With your finger, trace along the grid to the point where the two centers meet. Compare a symbol at the center of the chart to the key and choose which floss color to stitch first. To find the center of the fabric, fold it into quarters and finger-crease.

Cut the floss into 15" lengths and separate all six strands. Recombine the appropriate number of strands and thread them into a blunt-tip needle. Unless otherwise indicated, use two strands of floss to work cross stitches, half cross stitches, and quarter cross stitches. Use one strand of floss to work backstitches and French knots.

To Secure Thread at the Beginning

The most common way to secure the beginning tail of the thread is to hold it on the wrong side of the fabric under the first four or five stitches.

To Secure Thread at the End

To finish, slip the threaded needle under previously stitched threads on the wrong side of the fabric for four or five stitches, weaving the thread back and forth a few times. Clip the thread.

Cross Stitch

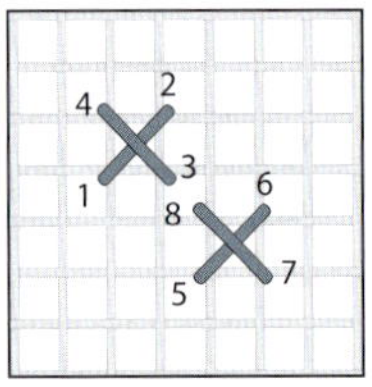

Make one cross stitch for each symbol on the chart. For horizontal rows, stitch the first diagonal of each stitch in the row. Work back across the row, completing each stitch. On linen and evenweave fabrics, work the stitches over two threads as shown in the diagram. For aida cloth, each stitch fills one square. You also can work cross stitches in the reverse direction. Remember to embroider the stitches uniformly—that is, always work the top half of each stitch in the same direction.

Half Cross Stitches

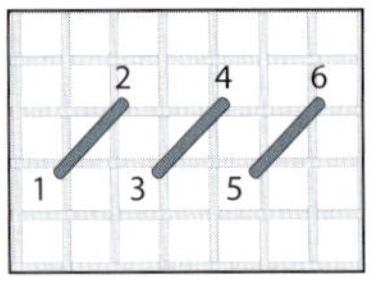

A half cross stitch is a single diagonal or half a cross stitch. They are indicated on the chart by a diagonal colored symbol.

Backstitches

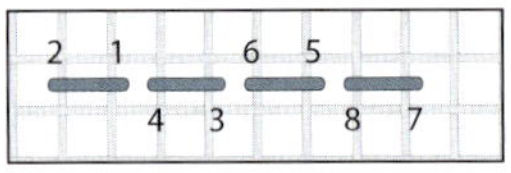

Working from right to left, bring the needle up from the back side of the fabric, one stitch length from your starting point. Begin the next stitch by inserting the needle at your starting point and back up two stitch lengths away. Continue, keeping all the stitches the same length.

French Knot

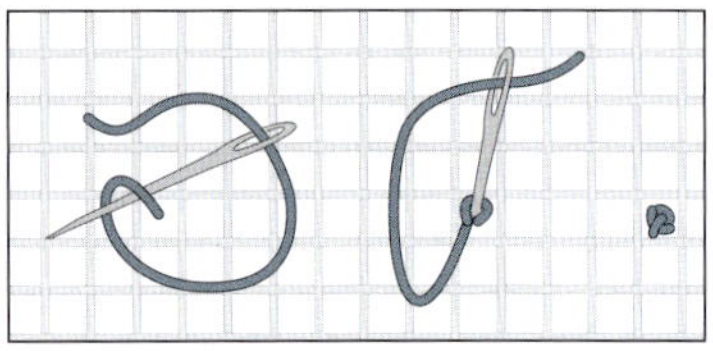

Bring the threaded needle through the fabric and wrap the floss around the needle as shown. Tighten the twists and return the needle through the fabric in the same place. The floss will slide through the wrapped thread to make the knot.

Quarter Cross Stitches

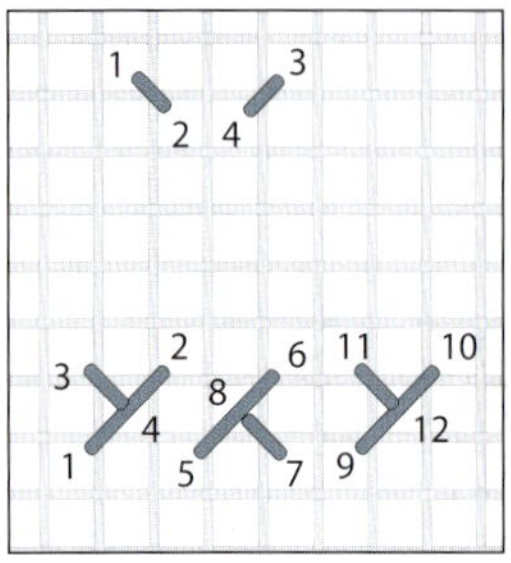

To obtain rounded shapes in a design, use quarter and three-quarter cross stitches. On linen and evenweave fabrics, a quarter stitch will extend from the corner to the center intersection of the threads. To make quarter cross stitches on aida cloth, estimate the center of the square. Three-quarter cross stitches combine a quarter cross stitch with a half cross stitch. Both stitches may slant in any direction.

Cross Stitch With Beads

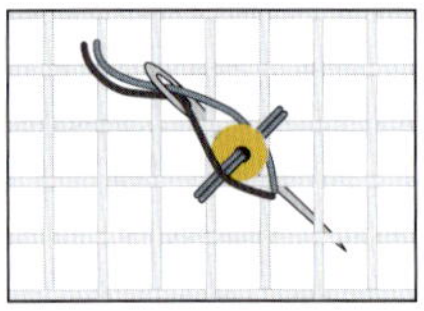

Beads can be attached by working the first half of each cross stitch and attaching a bead on the return stitch (use one strand of floss). Another method—to ensure that beads stand up straight—is to work with two strands of floss and add the bead to the first half stitch. As you work the second diagonal, split the strands so one strand lies on each side of the bead.

Produced by Herrschners, Inc., for distribution exclusively by Leisure Arts, Inc., 104 Champs Blvd., STE 100, Maumelle, AR 72113-6738, leisurearts.com.